THE GIFT OF THE NUTCRACKER
LEADER GUIDE

The Gift of the Nutcracker

The Gift of the Nutcracker
978-1-5018-6942-6
978-1-5018-6943-3 eBook
978-1-5018-7614-1 Large Print

The Gift of the Nutcracker / DVD
978-1-5018-6946-4

The Gift of the Nutcracker / Leader Guide
978-1-5018-6944-0
978-1-5018-6945-7 eBook

The Gift of the Nutcracker / Youth Study Book
978-1-5018-6951-8
978-1-5018-6952-5 eBook

The Gift of the Nutcracker / Children's Leader Guide
978-1-5018-7151-1

The Gift of the Nutcracker / Worship Resources
978-1-5018-6953-2 Flash Drive
978-1-5018-6954-9 Download

The Gift of the Nutcracker / Leader Kit
978-1-5018-7618-9

Also by Matt Rawle

The Faith of a Mockingbird
Hollywood Jesus
The Salvation of Doctor Who
The Redemption of Scrooge
What Makes a Hero?

with Juan Huertas and Katie McKay-Simpson
The Marks of Hope: Where the Spirit Is Moving in a Wounded Church

MATT RAWLE

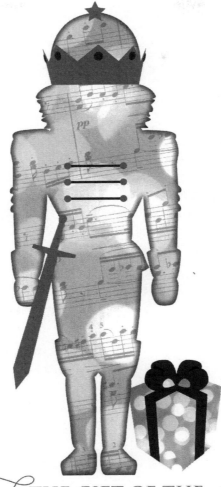

THE GIFT OF THE
Nutcracker

LEADER GUIDE BY MARTHA BETTIS GEE

Abingdon Press / Nashville

The Gift of the Nutcracker
Leader Guide

978-1-5018-6944-0

Scripture quotations, unless noted otherwise, are taken from the New Revised Standard Version of the Bible, copyright 1989, Division of Christian Education of the National Council of the Churches of Christ in the United States of America. Used by permission. All rights reserved.

18 19 20 21 22 23 24 25 26 27 — 10 9 8 7 6 5 4 3 2 1
MANUFACTURED IN THE UNITED STATES OF AMERICA

CONTENTS

To the Leader 7

1. Clara: Waiting for Christmas 12

2. Drosselmeir: A Godfather's Love................. 25

3. The Mouse King: Changing Perspective 37

4. The Nutcracker: The Greatest Gift............... 51

Appendix...................................... 62

TO THE LEADER

Welcome! In this study, you have the opportunity to help a group of learners explore what the story of *The Nutcracker* reveals about the gift of Jesus Christ. The study is based on the book *The Gift of the Nutcracker*.

Matt Rawle, the author of the study, is the lead pastor at Asbury United Methodist Church in Bossier City, Louisiana, and a graduate of the LSU School of Music and Duke Divinity School. Rawle describes himself as a speaker who loves to tell an old story in a new way, especially at the intersection of pop culture and the church. For many people, attending a performance of *The Nutcracker* ballet is a highlight of the Christmas season. Rawle invites us to encounter anew the old, old story of Jesus' birth as we experience, through a twelve-year-old's imagination and a godfather's great love, the defeat of a mouse king and the gift of a nutcracker who becomes real. In the process, we have the opportunity to discover the beauty of God's greatest gift to us—the gift of Jesus.

Scripture tells us that where two or three are gathered together in Jesus' name, we can be assured of the presence of the Holy Spirit, working in and through all those gathered. As you prepare to lead, pray for that presence and expect that you will experience it.

The study includes four sessions, and it makes use of the following components:

- The book *The Gift of the Nutcracker* by Matt Rawle;
- the DVD that accompanies the study;
- this Leader Guide.

Participants in the study will also need Bibles, as well as either a spiral-bound notebook for a journal or an electronic means of journaling, such as a tablet. If possible, notify those interested in the study in advance of the first session. Make arrangements for them to get copies of the book so that they can read the Introduction and Chapter 1 before the first group meeting.

USING THIS GUIDE WITH YOUR GROUP

Because no two groups are alike, this guide has been designed to give you flexibility and choice in tailoring the sessions for your group. The session format is listed below. You may choose any or all of the activities, adapting them as you wish to meet the schedule and needs of your particular group.

This leader guide offers a basic session plan designed to be completed in a session of about 45 minutes. Select ahead of time which activities the group will do, for how long, and in what order. Depending on which activities you select, there may be special preparation needed. The leader is alerted in the session plan when advance preparation is needed.

Session Format

Planning the Session

Session Goals
Scriptural Foundation
Special Preparation

Getting Started

> Opening Activity
> Opening Prayer

Learning Together

> Video Study and Discussion
> Book and Bible Study and Discussion
> More Activities (Optional)

Wrapping Up

> Closing Activity
> Closing Prayer

Helpful Hints

Preparing for the Session

- Pray for the leading of the Holy Spirit as you prepare for the study. Pray for discernment for yourself and for each member of the study group.
- Before each session, familiarize yourself with the content. Read the book chapter again.
- Choose the session elements you will use during the group session, including the specific discussion questions you plan to cover. Be prepared, however, to adjust the session as group members interact and as questions arise. Prepare carefully, but allow space for the Holy Spirit to move in and through the group members and through you as facilitator.
- Prepare the room where the group will meet so that the space will enhance the learning process. Ideally, group members should be seated around a table or in a circle so

that all can see each other. Movable chairs are best because the group will often be forming pairs or small groups for discussion.

- Bring a supply of Bibles for those who forget to bring their own. Also bring writing paper and pens or pencils for those participants who do not bring a journal or a tablet or other electronic means of journaling.
- For most sessions you will also need a chalkboard and chalk, a whiteboard and markers, or an easel with large sheets of paper and markers.

Shaping the Learning Environment

- Begin on time.
- Create a climate of openness, encouraging group members to participate as they feel comfortable.
- Remember that some people will jump right in with answers and comments, while others need time to process what is being discussed.
- If you notice that some group members seem never to be able to enter the conversation, ask them if they have thoughts to share. Give everyone a chance to talk, but keep the conversation moving. Moderate to prevent a few individuals from doing all the talking.
- Communicate the importance of group discussions and group exercises.
- If no one answers at first during discussions, do not be afraid of silence. Count silently to ten, then say something such as, "Would anyone like to go first?" If no one responds, venture an answer yourself and ask for comments.
- Model openness as you share with the group. Group members will follow your example. If you limit your sharing to a surface level, others will follow suit.

- Encourage multiple answers or responses before moving on to the next question.
- To help continue a discussion and give it greater depth, ask, "Why?" or "Why do you believe that?" or "Can you say more about that?"
- Affirm others' responses with comments such as "Great" or "Thanks" or "Good insight," especially if it's the first time someone has spoken during the group session.
- Monitor your own contributions. If you are doing most of the talking, back off so that you do not train the group to listen rather than speak up.
- Remember that you do not have all the answers. Your job is to keep the discussion going and encourage participation.

Managing the Session

- Honor the time schedule. If a session is running longer than expected, get consensus from the group before continuing beyond the agreed-upon ending time.
- Involve group members in various aspects of the group session, such as saying prayers or reading Scripture.
- Note that the session guides sometimes call for breaking into smaller groups or pairs. This gives everyone a chance to speak and participate fully. Mix up the groups; don't let the same people pair up for every activity.
- As always in discussions that may involve personal sharing, confidentiality is essential. Group members should never pass along stories that have been shared in the group. Remind the group members at each session: confidentiality is crucial to the success of this study.

Session 1

CLARA: WAITING FOR CHRISTMAS

PLANNING THE SESSION

Session Goals

As a result of conversations and activities connected with this session, group members should explore, through the lens of Scripture, what *The Nutcracker* reveals about the gift of Jesus Christ by beginning to:

- consider anticipation and curiosity;
- examine the dynamics of in-between time;
- encounter surprise and suspense;
- reflect on signs of Advent.

Scriptural Foundation

The days are surely coming, says the LORD, when I will fulfill the promise I made to the house of

Israel and the house of Judah. In those days and at that time I will cause a righteous Branch to spring up for David; and he shall execute justice and righteousness in the land. In those days Judah will be saved and Jerusalem will live in safety. And this is the name by which it will be called: 'The LORD is our righteousness.'

Jeremiah 33:14-16

"Do not be afraid, Mary, for you have found favor with God. And now, you will conceive in your womb and bear a son, and you will name him Jesus. He will be great, and will be called the Son of the Most High, and the Lord God will give to him the throne of his ancestor David. He will reign over the house of Jacob forever, and of his kingdom there will be no end."

Luke 1:30–33

Now every year his parents went to Jerusalem for the festival of the Passover. And when he was twelve years old, they went up as usual for the festival. When the festival was ended and they started to return, the boy Jesus stayed behind in Jerusalem, but his parents did not know it. Assuming that he was in the group of travelers, they went a day's journey. Then they started to look for him among their relatives and friends. When they did not find him, they returned to Jerusalem to search for him. After three days they found him in the temple, sitting among the teachers, listening to them and asking them questions. And all who heard him were amazed at his understanding and his answers. When his parents saw him they were astonished; and his mother said to him, "Child, why have you treated

13

us like this? Look, your father and I have been searching for you in great anxiety." He said to them, "Why were you searching for me? Did you not know that I must be in my Father's house?" But they did not understand what he said to them. Then he went down with them and came to Nazareth, and was obedient to them. His mother treasured all these things in her heart.

And Jesus increased in wisdom and in years, and in divine and human favor.

Luke 2:41-52

Special Preparation

- If participants are not familiar with one another, provide nametags.
- Have available a notebook or paper and pen or pencil for anyone who did not bring a notebook or an electronic device for journaling.
- Decide if you will use any of the optional activities. For the activity of looking through a keyhole, you will need to cut simple keyhole shapes in sheets of printing or drawing paper for each participant. To view portions of *The Nutcracker* ballet, download selected segments from the Internet and obtain equipment for viewing.
- Decide if you will sing an Advent carol. Choose one familiar to your group, perhaps a carol with the theme of preparation or anticipation, such as "O Come, O Come, Emmanuel."
- For the closing activity in all four sessions, you will need four Advent candles, typically purple. You may want to

set up an Advent wreath, or simply have four candles in a single line. Electronic candles are a good alternative if your church has restrictions about lighting conventional candles. Note: Advent candles are assigned a theme each week, although for most denominations there is no hard and fast rule about which candle bears which designation. In this study, the author has chosen to begin with the candle of peace, and then to continue with hope, love, and joy.

GETTING STARTED

Opening Activity

As participants arrive, welcome them to the study. When most participants have arrived, invite them to form pairs and discuss together a time when they were in the audience awaiting the beginning of a performance, whether of *The Nutcracker* or of some other play, concert, or ballet. What do they remember feeling? What was happening around them in the audience?

After allowing a few minutes for pairs to discuss, ask each person to respond in turn to the following:

My name is _____ and here's what I remember about how I felt as I waited for the performance to begin…

Tell the group that in this study, they will have the opportunity to explore a familiar Christmas tradition, *The Nutcracker* story, and what it might reveal about the gift of Jesus Christ. In this session, they will begin to explore the world of *The Nutcracker* through the eyes of twelve-year-old Clara.

Opening Prayer

Pray the following prayer, or one of your own choosing:

Holy God, as we prepare for the coming of your Son, Jesus, at Christmas, quiet us down. By your Spirit, open our hearts, our minds, and our wills to what you would reveal to us through your story as it is told in Scripture and in the story of The Nutcracker. *Amen.*

LEARNING TOGETHER

Video Study and Discussion

In Chapter 1, we are introduced to *The Nutcracker*—the ballet whose music and story are a beloved Christmas tradition for many. Matt Rawle, the author of the study, is the lead pastor at Asbury United Methodist Church in Bossier City, Louisiana, and a graduate of the LSU School of Music and Duke Divinity School. Rawle describes himself as a speaker who loves to tell an old story in a new way, especially at the intersection of pop culture and the church.

We begin by exploring the world through the eyes of twelve-year-old Clara, who peeks through a keyhole to gaze longingly on the Christmas tree that is the center of the party for adults. When Clara is allowed to join the party, she receives a nutcracker from her godfather—a gift around which the ensuing story centers. After viewing the video segment, discuss some of the following:

- Matt Rawle observes that one way to look at this story is to make a connection between Advent and Clara's experience of brokenness. What does he mean?

- He notes that there can be a disconnect between expectation and reality. How is this played out in *The Nutcracker*? What aspects of the Christmas story illustrate such a disconnect? Where, if at all, have you experienced this in your own life?
- We hear that Advent is a time of awaiting Christ, preparing yourself for this greatest gift of God. But it's also a time of recognizing that this work is not yet complete. What examples can you give of places in the life of your community, the nation, or the world, where the work of the hands and feet of people of faith is still needed?

Book and Bible Study and Discussion

Consider Anticipation and Curiosity

Invite a volunteer to read aloud Jeremiah 33:14-16, one of this session's focus scriptures. Discuss some of the following:

- The author observes that anticipation and curiosity go hand in hand. How does he explain this? Would you agree? Why or why not? When have you experienced anticipation before an event or an evolving situation? Were you curious about the outcome?
- Is your sense of curiosity different if you are awaiting something with dread instead of anticipation? If so, how?
- How does the author suggest that Advent anticipation is unique?
- What function does light serve in the season of Advent?
- Respond to the following questions posed by the author: "How do you use light in your Christmas decorations? How do you tell Christ's story through light?"

Examine the Dynamics of "In-Between" Time

Ask someone to read aloud Luke 2:41-52, another of this session's focus scriptures. Discuss the following:

- The author notes that the point in Luke's story of Jesus' adolescence is how "in between" isn't either/or, but both/and. What does he mean by that? How do you respond?
- He reminds us that "being 'in between' is always where we find ourselves." In what ways, if at all, do you find yourself "in between" in the sense that Rawle suggests? What spiritual practices do you find helpful in searching, learning, and growing?

According to Matt Rawle, our Christmas traditions help ground us in our "in-between" lives. Form pairs or small groups, depending on the size of your group. In these smaller groupings, invite participants to discuss the following questions he poses:

- What are some of the traditions you most look forward to each year?
- Where do those traditions take place? Do they happen inside your home, or while you are visiting friends and family? In the sanctuary? Somewhere else?
- Do you greet the days of preparation with eager anticipation, or with some other emotions? Why? How do you feel about Christmas Eve?

After allowing several minutes for pairs or small groups to discuss, come together in the total group. Invite each pair or group to report on what came out of their discussion about the final questions that addressed anticipation and other emotions.

Ask someone to briefly describe what happens when Clara is allowed to enter the Christmas party. What special gift does she receive, and from whom? What happens to it? Ask volunteers to respond to the following:

- Describe an episode in your life when you experienced unmet expectations, or when something you'd been looking forward to went horribly wrong. Did you experience panic, fear, anger, or disappointment? Some other emotion?
- The author asks us to consider the possibility that "sometimes when things go wrong we even discover a new, more helpful perspective." What do you think? Has this ever been your experience? If so, what was the outcome?
- In speaking of traditions, he observes that the only thing constant is change. What do our Advent traditions reveal about what that constant is for people of faith?

Encounter Surprise and Suspense

Pose the following questions for the group, and invite one or more volunteers to respond:

- Have you ever endured sleepless nights? If so, what were the circumstances?
- Were you having trouble going to sleep because you were anticipating something positive and exciting, or because of nervousness and anxiety about an upcoming challenge or a difficult situation?

In the ballet, the children retire for bed after the guests leave. The author suggests that Clara has trouble falling asleep; after checking on her nutcracker one more time, Clara falls asleep under the Christmas tree. But she is awakened by a disturbing dream.

19

Invite one or more volunteers to read aloud Luke 1:26-38, the passage in which another of this session's focus scriptures is found. Discuss some of the following:

- The author suggests that "the story of Jesus' birth sounds like a story about sleepless nights." Why do you think he characterizes it in this way?
- He notes that "we aren't told why Mary greeted God's word with affirmation," and poses some possible reactions Mary might have had to Gabriel's surprising news. Why do you think Mary responded affirmatively? Given the circumstances in which she found herself, how do you imagine she might have been feeling?
- Matt Rawle tells us that one of his clergy friends "often says that God's middle name is Surprise, but I'm beginning to believe that God's middle name is Suspense." Where do you see evidence of surprise in the stories of Jesus' birth from Luke and Matthew? Where do you find suspense?
- The author points out that we do not hear Mary's voice in Matthew's account, nor do we hear Joseph's in Luke. What does he suggest is the reason for their silence? Do you agree with his stated reason, or can you suggest other reasons?

Reflect on Signs of Advent

We read that Clara's dream quickly turns into a nightmare, but the Nutcracker comes to her defense against the giant mice at the last moment. The author invites us to consider if she might have been "so focused on the mice closing in on her that she missed that the Nutcracker was there the whole time."

Remind the group that when the angels appeared to the shepherds, they pointed to a sign that would reveal the truth of

Jesus' birth. The author suggests that when we are inspired by the Holy Spirit "to take risks, to pick up the cross, and to step out in faith, God will always supply a sign, a touchstone, or something tangible to affirm our conviction." Yet we must take care about which signs we heed. Invite participants to focus on what tools they use in seeking discernment about how to better follow Jesus.

Ask them to reflect on the following questions that relate to ideas they have considered in this session and respond in writing in their journals:

- What spiritual tools can I employ to align my life more completely to God's purpose in the world, as revealed in the life of Jesus Christ?
- How do I enhance a continuing spirit of curiosity and anticipation for God's wonderful work?
- What spiritual practices might help me further increase and become strong in wisdom in this in-between time of growth?
- How do the traditions my family cherishes contribute to a sense of preparation for the coming of Christ anew in the world? Are there traditions that drain instead of energize our lives during this time? Do we need to let go of some traditions and embrace others that are more life-giving?

Encourage participants to continue to reflect on these questions and others that arise in the coming week. Suggest that they commit to a renewed emphasis on a spiritual practice such as reading Scripture or engaging in regular prayer. For some participants who are not already setting aside time for devotions, this hectic season may not be conducive to beginning. In that case, suggest that they set aside a brief period of time daily for quiet meditation, simply praying "Come, Lord Jesus."

More Activities (Optional)

View a Segment of The Nutcracker

If there are those in your group who are less than familiar with the story of the ballet, help participants enter the story by downloading and viewing a segment of Act 1 of *The Nutcracker* from the Internet.

Visualize the World through a Keyhole

Remind the group that at the beginning of the story of *The Nutcracker*, the young girl Clara peeks through a keyhole from the family drawing room to see if she can catch sight of what's happening on the other side of the locked door. She can catch only fleeting glimpses of the festivities.

Distribute the sheets of paper prepared with keyhole cutouts. Invite group members to hold up the sheets and look through the keyhole shape. Then invite volunteers to imagine that they have not seen the space where you are meeting and are not familiar with its furnishings. Ask volunteers to tell how they would describe the space, based only on what they can see through the keyhole.

Acknowledge that most participants who have been in this learning space before can extrapolate what is in the room based on their previous experiences there. Likewise, in Advent our anticipation is not about the story of Jesus' birth, with which we are already familiar. The author observes that Advent is different in the sense that "our thankfulness is overshadowed by an anticipation born out of curiosity over how a child wrapped in swaddling clothes will save our souls and continue to transform the world." He notes that perhaps we might channel that sense of anticipation as a continuing "spirit of curiosity and anticipation for God's wonderful and amazing work."

Ask that participants consider places in their family, the community, our nation, and the world where God's healing work is needed. Ask them to reflect on those wounded places and choose one on which to place their focus. Have them write that issue or situation on the keyhole sheet, then think about what they can observe about it based on their limited present view—what they could see from simply getting a "keyhole" glimpse—and jot down phrases describing that glimpse.

Encourage them to consider opening the imaginary door to reveal more by doing some research on how God's healing hand might be needed, and to commit to taking one step toward being God's hands and feet in the world.

Give Voice to Mary and Joseph

Invite group members to take the role of either Mary or Joseph. Using the Scripture passages from Luke and Matthew, ask them to write a short entry in their journals describing how they feel about the impending birth of the Messiah. What fears and apprehensions are theirs? What hopes? How do they anticipate this news will be taken by friends and family? After allowing a few minutes for participants to write, invite one or more volunteers to read their entries.

WRAPPING UP

Point out that the author tells us that "Advent rests in the tension-filled space between Jesus' birth and his continuous work that propels us into the future." In that sense, "Advent is always." Invite participants who choose to do so to respond, popcorn style, to the following:

In the tension-filled space of Advent, and in the in-between space of my life, I will remember Jesus' birth by _____ .

In the tension-filled space of Advent, and in the in-between space of my life, I will seek to discern how to be a part of Christ's continuous work by _____ .

Remind participants to read Chapter 2 before the next session.

Closing Activity

Light a Candle and Sing a Hymn

Light the first of the four candles and sit in silence for a few moments. Then say, "Come, Lord Jesus." Sing together the Advent carol of your choice.

Closing Prayer

Pray the following, or a prayer of your choosing:

Come, Lord Jesus. As we await your coming anew into the world at Christmas, we seek to enter ever more deeply into what Scripture has to reveal. With anticipation, we open ourselves to new insights. With curiosity, we seek discernment about what you have in store for us today and in the coming weeks. With thanksgiving, we affirm our role in your transforming work. Amen.

Session 2

DROSSELMEIR: A GODFATHER'S LOVE

PLANNING THE SESSION

Session Goals

As a result of conversations and activities connected with this session, group members should explore, through the lens of Scripture, what *The Nutcracker* reveals about the gift of Jesus Christ by beginning to:

- encounter words of comfort and hope in biblical prophecy;
- examine, through Drosselmeir's puppet show, what prophecy is—and is not;
- consider the meaning and implications of God's grace;
- reflect on God's presence in Advent.

Scriptural Foundation

Comfort, O comfort my people,
*   says your God.*
Speak tenderly to Jerusalem,
*   and cry to her*
that she has served her term,
*   that her penalty is paid,*
that she has received from the LORD's hand
*   double for all her sins.*

A voice cries out:
"In the wilderness prepare the way of the LORD,
*   make straight in the desert a highway for*
*   our God.*
Every valley shall be lifted up,
*   and every mountain and hill be made low;*
the uneven ground shall become level,
*   and the rough places a plain.*
Then the glory of the LORD shall be revealed,
*   and all people shall see it together,*
*   for the mouth of the LORD has spoken."*

Isaiah 40:1-5

Mary said to the angel, "How can this be, since
I am a virgin?" The angel said to her, "The Holy
Spirit will come upon you, and the power of the
Most High will overshadow you; therefore the
child to be born will be holy; he will be called Son
of God. And now, your relative Elizabeth in her
old age has also conceived a son; and this is the
sixth month for her who was said to be barren. For
nothing will be impossible with God." Then Mary
said, "Here am I, the servant of the Lord; let it be
with me according to your word." Then the angel
departed from her.

Luke 1:34-38

Special Preparation

- Continue to have available a notebook or paper and pen or pencil for anyone who did not bring a notebook or an electronic device for journaling.

- For the opening activity, print the words "Be Not Afraid" on a large sheet of paper or a board.

- For the activity on exploring words of comfort and hope, print the following on a large sheet of paper or a board: In our contemporary context: What situations or experiences constitute wilderness? What might it mean to prepare the way of the Lord in our wilderness experiences? How does our experience of God change as our relationship with the Holy One deepens?

- Decide if you will use any of the optional additional activities. To again view portions of *The Nutcracker* ballet, download selected segments from the internet and obtain the equipment for viewing.

- For the closing activity, decide if you will sing the Advent carol "The Lord Is My Light." Obtain the lyrics and arrange for accompaniment. If your group is unfamiliar with the carol, you could simply plan to view a video segment, or you could obtain the lyrics and have the group read them aloud, either in unison or by having a different volunteer read each stanza.

- You will again need four Advent candles, either in an Advent wreath or simply standing in a line. Electronic candles are a good alternative if your church has restrictions about lighting conventional candles.

Getting Started

Opening Activity

As participants arrive, welcome them. Invite volunteers who were present for the first session to describe any actions they took during the past week to focus on a spiritual practice. Also invite participants who evaluated their Christmas traditions to report on any tradition they determined was more life-draining than life-enhancing. In what ways might they either transform that tradition or replace it with another?

As a way of reviewing and to help those who were not present in the first session get up to speed, ask participants to name in turn the events of the first act of *The Nutcracker*. Begin by saying, "Clara peeks through the keyhole in the door, observing the adults enjoying the festivities." Ask participants to add other details until the act has been described.

Call the group's attention to the phrase "Be not afraid" that you posted. Ask participants to respond, popcorn style, to the following:

- Think about the current context in which we are living in our community, the nation, or the world. What situations or crises might lead you to be fearful?

After allowing time for response, remind the group that the children in the story were initially fearful of the cloaked figure of Drosselmeir. Tell them that in this session, they will explore more fully who Drosselmeir is, what role he plays, and who he might represent.

Opening Prayer

Pray the following prayer, or one of your own choosing:

Gracious God, as we come together, we are reminded of your promise that wherever two or three are gathered in Jesus' name, there your Spirit will be also. Make us ever more deeply aware of your presence, both in our midst today and throughout this season of Advent. Amen.

LEARNING TOGETHER

Video Study and Discussion

In Chapter 2, we explore more deeply the character of Clara's godfather, Drosselmeir. Through the puppet show, as in biblical prophecy, we discover some, although not all, of what is about to unfold. Through Drosselmeir's gift of the nutcracker, we explore the gift of God's grace, and we discover who is at the center of the story, regardless of the perspective from which we are viewing it. After viewing the video segment, discuss some of the following:

We hear of two of the author's friends who received Christmas gifts. Each friend was initially less than thrilled about the gift, but both later altered that first impression. When, if ever, have you had this experience? What happened to change your first impression of the desirability of the gift?

- The author describes Clara's godfather, Drosselmeir, as a divine figure who represents God. What details about Drosselmeir does he cite to support this idea? How do you respond?
- What comparisons does he make between Old Testament prophecies and Drosselmeir's puppet show? What does this reveal about the nature of prophecy?

- When Clara is not quite sure if the nutcracker is a good gift or a bad gift, Drosselmeir shows her what it is and how to use it. What sign does Gabriel offer to Mary in the face of her uncertainty at his announcement?
- The author observes that when God asks us to do something, God always offers us a sign. What does he suggest that sign is? When and in what ways have you experienced God's presence when you have discerned a particular call to discipleship?

Book and Bible Study and Discussion

Encounter Words of Comfort and Hope

The author tells us that a word from God offers the "assurance of God's presence and a hope for the future" but also provides an "example of how God desires us to respond in times of great tragedy and grief." Invite one or more volunteers to read aloud Isaiah 40:1-5, one of this session's foundational scriptures.

Call the group's attention to the three questions you posted. Form three small groups and assign one question to each. After allowing time for the groups to work, invite each one to report to the total group on their discussion.

Point out that the groups or pairs who discussed the questions did so in isolation from one another, so that the discussion of preparation in wilderness experiences probably did not deal with the specifics of a particular experience. Invite participants to choose one of the experiences identified by the first group and brainstorm ways to prepare for Jesus' coming in that situation.

Ask a volunteer to read Luke 1:34-38, another of this session's foundational scriptures and a continuation of one of last session's passages. Discuss the following:

- The author describes Mary's first reply to the angel as a "your God" kind of moment, and her last response to the angel as an "our God" moment. What does he mean?

Examine What Prophecy Is—and Is Not

Ask someone to briefly describe the storyline of the puppet show. Point out that the author tells us that "the puppet show offers us a picture of what prophecy is," and equally important, "what prophecy is not." Jot down two headings on a board or a large sheet of paper—"Is" and "Is Not." First invite the group to name characteristics of what prophecy *is*, according to the author, and jot these down under the first heading. Then repeat the process for characteristics of what prophecy *is not*, and record these under the other heading. Discuss:

- What reasons are we given for the fact that prophecies are often characterized by vagueness?
- We read that Scripture doesn't tell us everything we want to know, but it does reveal everything we need. How do you respond? Would you agree? Why or why not?

Consider the Meaning and Implications of God's Grace

After the puppet show, Drosselmeir presents the children with other gifts (a ballerina, a clown, and a sugar plum fairy) who dance as if they are alive. The author observes that in a way, "the prophecies about the coming Messiah become so full of God's Holy Spirit that they come alive in the person of Jesus." He asserts that the key concept linking God and Jesus is grace, God's gift.

Divide participants into three pairs or small groups, depending on the size of your group, preferably with participants in different groupings from the previous activity. To each pair or small group, assign one of the three distinct ways to think about grace: grace as a gift offered; grace as a gift received; grace as a gift shared. Encourage participants to visualize this gift using the metaphor the author uses: as a gift under the Christmas tree. Ask them to read what the text has to say about their group's aspect of grace, and to discuss its implications together.

After allowing groups or pairs to work, ask each group to report their conversation, as well as any key points or questions that surfaced. To extend the conversation, discuss the following:

- How does the author define prevenient, justifying, and sanctifying grace?
- Describe what happens when Fritz, who believes he should have the gift, tries to take the nutcracker away from Clara. What happens when we view grace as something we deserve? How might this alter the way we approach grace?
- What does the author identify as "an exercise in grace offered, received, and shared"? How, if at all, have you experienced it in this way?

Reflect on God's Presence in Advent

Invite participants to review the information in the text about healing. We read that Drosselmeir "heals" the nutcracker (repairs it) before disappearing for a time from the storyline. In observing that healing can be complicated, the author poses the question: "If Drosselmeir can mend a nutcracker, why does he disappear when Clara is threatened by the Mouse King?" Invite one or two volunteers to describe times when they or someone they know was in need of healing and God seemed very far away. What happened?

Matt Rawle tells us that despite Drosselmeir's absence at some key moments of *The Nutcracker*, he is nevertheless there at the beginning, in the middle, and at the ending of the story. Likewise, Scripture talks about God as one who is, was, and is to come. Invite participants to reflect on the following and respond to one or more of the questions in writing in their journals.

- The God *who was* means that we are forgiven. How and in what situations have you experienced God's forgiveness?
- The God *who is* embodies the present tense, the God who loves us. In what ways, if at all, have you personally experienced God as present? In what situations have you had a strong sense that God has not abandoned you, regardless of the outcomes? Conversely, has there ever been a time when you felt abandoned by God? What was the situation? What happened?
- A God *who is to come* means that God can be trusted. When and in what ways have you discerned what your purpose might be for God's kingdom? If your sense of purpose is less than clear, what tools might you employ in order to continue to discern how you fit into God's loving purpose for the cosmos? Where do you feel called to serve God?

Encourage participants to open themselves in the coming week to a stronger sense of God's presence in their past, their present, and their future. In addition to times of prayer, meditation, and Scripture reading in the days to come, suggest that they intentionally pause in their daily routine, stopping to try to more clearly discern God's presence.

More Activities (Optional)

View a Segment of The Nutcracker

For those not familiar with *The Nutcracker*, view segments of the ballet on the Internet, such as one showing Drosselmeir's entrance. If there are those who were not present for the previous session, you may want to view some of the segments suggested for Session 1.

Explore Healing Stories in John

Point out that Matt Rawle invites us to expand our understanding of the healing light of Jesus come into the world through examining the healing of the broken nutcracker. Form four pairs or small groups, depending on the size of your group. Assign one of the following ways that Jesus heals to each pair or small group: destroying false assumptions; restoring dignity; dissolving fear; healing our faith. Ask each pair or group to read John 9 and the material in the text about their assigned way of healing, then discuss together.

After allowing a few minutes for pairs or groups to work, come together in the total group and invite them to report on their discussions. Then discuss the following together:

- The author tells us that Drosselmeir's absence following his repair of the nutcracker points us to a profound truth about healing. What is it? How do you respond?

Consider Different Perspectives

The author observes that *The Nutcracker* is Drosselmeir's story told through Clara's eyes. He poses the question: "Would the story change if we overheard it from another character's point of view?" Invite participants to choose one of the following characters and briefly jot down a few sentences describing how that character might tell the story:

- The Mouse King
- Fritz (Clara's brother)
- The Nutcracker

After a few minutes for writing, invite one or more volunteers to report. Ask:

- Do you think each of these characters would conclude that Drosselmeir is a loving godfather? Why or why not?

Suggest that participants now repeat the exercise, choosing one of the following characters from the Christmas story:

- Shepherds
- Mary
- Angels
- Joseph

Ask the group to respond to the following:

- Regardless of the perspective from which the story of *The Nutcracker* is told, who is the truth on which the story hangs?
- Who is the truth on which the story of Christmas is told?

WRAPPING UP

Remind participants that in Session 1, the author observed that in some ways "Advent is always," not just a season of time preceding Christmas. In Chapter 2, he tells us that in lighting one of the candles of Advent, the candle of peace, "we remind ourselves that we should be at peace all 365 days of the year." Real peace—Kingdom Peace—is a gift we yearn for.

As the group considered the gift of the nutcracker, they focused on how grace functions as a gift. Invite them now to imagine they are being presented with a beautifully wrapped gift. It might be the gift of grace, the gift of peace, or some other intangible yet profoundly important gift. Ask them to respond to the following:

If I could receive one gift in this season—a gift freely offered with no strings attached—it would be...

As a follower of Jesus Christ, I would seek to share this gift with others by...

Point out that the author tells us that the sacrament of Holy Communion "is an exercise in grace offered, received, and shared." Encourage participants to consider this sign of grace when next they receive Communion.

Remind participants to read Chapter 3 before the next session.

Closing Activity

Light a Candle and Sing a Hymn

Light two of the four candles and sit in silence for a few moments. Then say, "Come, Lord Jesus."

Point out that the author observes that "during the Advent and Christmas season, we often talk about Jesus' birth as a healing light entering into a world of darkness." The carol "The Lord Is My Light" expresses this idea. Sing the carol if you have decided to do so, or simply have the group view a video segment of the carol or read the stanzas aloud together.

Closing Prayer

Pray the following, or a prayer of your choosing:

Come, Lord Jesus. As we encounter the busyness and whirl of the holiday season, make us ever more aware of where the center of our story lies—in Jesus Christ, Your Son, who is Lord yesterday, today, and tomorrow. Surround us with true peace. Make us aware of signs of grace. In the name of Jesus, the Messiah, the child born in a stable. Amen.

Session 3

THE MOUSE KING: CHANGING PERSPECTIVE

PLANNING THE SESSION

Session Goals

As a result of conversations and activities connected with this session, group members should explore, through the lens of Scripture, what *The Nutcracker* reveals about the gift of Jesus Christ by beginning to:

- examine the power of perspective;
- consider battles real and perceived;
- confront power in the gospel story;
- reflect on welcoming love as a guest in Advent.

Scriptural Foundation

> *In those days a decree went out from Emperor Augustus that all the world should be registered.*

This was the first registration and was taken while Quirinius was governor of Syria.

Luke 2:1-2

In the time of King Herod, after Jesus was born in Bethlehem of Judea, wise men from the East came to Jerusalem, asking, "Where is the child who has been born king of the Jews? For we observed his star at its rising, and have come to pay him homage." When King Herod heard this, he was frightened, and all Jerusalem with him; and calling together all the chief priests and scribes of the people, he inquired of them where the Messiah was to be born. They told him, "In Bethlehem of Judea...."

Then Herod secretly called for the wise men and learned from them the exact time when the star had appeared. Then he sent them to Bethlehem, saying, "Go and search diligently for the child; and when you have found him, bring me word so that I may also go and pay him homage."

Matthew 2:1-5, 7-8

In the fifteenth year of the reign of Emperor Tiberius, when Pontius Pilate was governor of Judea, and Herod was ruler of Galilee, and his brother Philip ruler of the region of Ituraea and Trachonitis, and Lysanias ruler of Abilene, during the high priesthood of Annas and Caiaphas, the word of God came to John son of Zechariah in the wilderness.

Luke 3:1-2

Special Preparation

- Have writing materials available for anyone who did not bring a journal.
- For the activity of considering real or perceived battles, print each of the following on a separate large sheet of paper: *Starbucks cup; "Christmas" versus "winter break"; taking "Christmas" off of sales-rack advertisements.* Post sheets at intervals around your space.
- For the reflecting activity, you may want to post the suggested questions for reflection on a large sheet of paper or a board.
- Decide if you will use any of the optional additional activities. To view portions of *The Nutcracker* ballet, download selected segments from the Internet and obtain equipment for viewing.
- For the closing activity, decide if you will sing the Advent carol "People, Look East." Obtain the lyrics and arrange for accompaniment. You could simply plan to view a video segment, or you could obtain the lyrics and have the group read them aloud, either in unison or by having a different volunteer read each stanza.
- You will again need four Advent candles, either in an Advent wreath or simply standing in a line. Electronic candles are a good alternative if your church has restrictions about lighting conventional candles.

GETTING STARTED

Opening Activity

Welcome participants. When most of the group has arrived, invite volunteers to describe any insights gleaned in the previous week from reflecting on God's presence in past, present, or future. Were there times when God seemed especially present? Times when it seemed as if God was very distant? Encourage the group to continue to look for signs of God's presence in the final weeks of Advent.

Invite participants to indicate, with a show of hands, if they are afraid of lizards or spiders. Ask those who indicated that they are afraid to respond to the following:

- What scares you about lizards or spiders?

Direct the following question to those who indicated no fear:

- Why are lizards or spiders not scary to you? Does their size have anything to do with it?
- What if you came across a giant lizard or a spider the size of an elephant? How would you feel then?

Point out that at the beginning of Chapter 3, Matt Rawle invites us to "think of old 1950s monster movies like *Tarantula*, *Godzilla*, and *The Blob*." When a lizard or other creature that we normally tower over is suddenly bigger than we are, we may experience fear.

Tell participants that in this session, they will explore how our perspective can alter the way we feel about an issue or a situation, as well as how we respond to it. Perspective matters, whether it has to do with the Mouse King or the sins of the world.

Opening Prayer

Pray the following prayer, or one of your own choosing:

Eternal God, as we encounter you once again in your word, give us new eyes and fresh perspectives. Remind us of the power of your community of believers gathered together. Rekindle our will that together we may respond to what you would have us do to more fully follow Jesus Christ, your Son, whose birth we anticipate. Amen.

LEARNING TOGETHER

Video Study and Discussion

In Chapter 3, we encounter the idea that perspective matters, whether in how Clara views the Mouse King, in the significance of the hierarchy of power we see represented in the scriptural story of Jesus' birth, or in our own perspectives on the problems of the world. The battle with the Mouse King reminds us that there is a cost involved in confronting powers and principalities. The good news of the Christ Child—news we are called to share—is that grace is freely offered in Christ's life and death. Yet sharing it with the world means that our love for the things that distract us from God's love must be crucified with Christ.

After viewing the video segment, discuss some of the following:

- The author notes that in Clara's dream the Mouse King might represent Fritz, her brother, who wrestled the nutcracker away from her. What does he suggest the Mouse King could represent to us? What is your own perspective on the world? Do you view the world as threatening, or are you able to consider it as God's good creation, even with all its problems?
- Rawle invites us to further consider perspective, notably Luke's perspective on power. Name the hierarchy of power that we find in Luke 2. How is that hierarchy turned upside down with the angels' announcement?

- Briefly relate what happened with the Christmas tree in Rawle's church. What is the happy accident he describes? When, and in what circumstances, have you observed or been a part of a similar happy accident?

- In *The Nutcracker*, it seems that all hope is lost when Clara comes face to face with the Mouse King. But the Nutcracker and a group of toy soldiers come to her aid. Rawle observes that when we surround ourselves with a community of believers, it begins to change our perspective. In what ways, if at all, does this particular community of believers function in a similar way? When has your perspective been altered by this community? As a part of a study? In acts of mission or service? Some other way?

Book and Bible Study and Discussion

Examine the Power of Perspective

Invite a volunteer to briefly summarize what the author tells us about Walt Disney World. Ask those participants who have visited either Disney World or Disneyland to describe what they remember about the perspective there. Discuss some of the following:

- What is forced perspective? Describe a time when your perceptions were shaped so as to make you feel larger or more secure. What buildings have you been in that were designed to make you feel smaller and less significant?

- Has there been a time when your attention was forced in a certain direction, as on a Disney World ride? What did you observe? As you look back, what might have been hidden from your view, and to what end?

- Matt Rawle suggests that "the church uses a kind of forced perspective every time we...worship." What does he mean? How does worship in our church shape our perceptions? Are there aspects of our worship where our message is confused? If so, where do you think we are communicating unintended messages?
- He observes that "sin forces our perspective in thinking that poverty is too big, homelessness is too pervasive, and problems are solved through legislation, petitions, or words in a Discipline." What does he suggest is necessary in order to put in proper perspective any of these or other challenges?
- What does the author mean when he asserts that Jesus is "God up close"? What impact might this have on the way we perceive the world's pressing problems?

Consider Battles Real and Perceived

We read that in the ballet, the Nutcracker's army and the Mouse King's troops are locked into a back-and-forth battle. At the end of the battle, both the Mouse King and the Nutcracker have been killed, although it's not entirely clear what they were fighting about.

Call the group's attention to the perennial seasonal battle in which we engage a range of issues around the importance of viewing the holiday season exclusively as the celebration of Christmas. Call attention to the three phrases you posted. Point out that they serve as a sort of shorthand for what some call "The War on Christmas." Invite each person to select one of the three phrases to discuss, and ask them to form groups around the selected posted phrase (if no one selects one of the choices, plan to discuss it briefly in the total group discussion). Ask each group to address the following in their discussion:

- Define the argument represented by the phrase.
- What is your position on this issue? Why?

In the total group, have each smaller group report on their discussion. Then discuss the following:

- Matt Rawle suggests that it's not nearly as important to say "Merry Christmas" as it is to do something else. What is it? How do you respond?
- He observes that "sometimes we confuse evangelism with apologetics." What does he mean? Which would you say is more important? Why?
- He notes that when we engage in defending ourselves against the War on Christmas, "our discipleship becomes defense without invitation, which means we build walls that end up protecting nothing." Do you agree? Why, or why not?

Confront Power in the Gospel Story

Invite volunteers to read aloud the two foundational scriptures for this session from Luke's Gospel. Discuss the following:

- After giving us an example of where real power rested with respect to the church prayer room, the author observes that "Luke offers a similar, yet more subtle, commentary on where power rests in the Gospel story." What does he suggest is revealed in these two accounts about where real power rests?

Ask a third volunteer to read aloud the Matthew passage. Ask:

- What does the author suggest is revealed about King Herod in this passage?

- What is the reason for King Herod's curiosity about the child? How does he respond to being thwarted in his quest to find the child?

Rawle observes that Herod was not aware that Jesus' goal was not to seek an earthly kingdom, but rather to establish God's realm here on earth. Invite participants to reflect in silence on the following:

- Who are the power brokers in our nation today? Are they the duly elected representatives of the people? Others of great power and wealth? Corporations? Some other person or entity?
- How do we, as followers of Christ, show our allegiance to a higher power, a greater and more enduring kingdom?

Remind the group of the discussion in the last session about grace. The author notes here that while "grace is freely offered,... receiving this grace, walking with it, sharing it with one another and the world means that our love for the things that distract us from God's love must be crucified with Christ." Invite participants to reflect in silence on the following:

- What habits or aspects of my life in this season—or in any season—distract me from God's love? Are there habits or perspectives I need to let go of in order to more completely be an agent of God's love in the world?
- What spiritual practices might enable me to be more acutely aware of the needs of my brothers and sisters?
- Rawle poses this question: "Is there a Mouse King in all of us that needs to be slain?" What do you think?

45

Invite volunteers to share insights they have about any or all of these questions.

Reflect on Welcoming Love as a Guest

Share the complete text of the hymn "People, Look East" (it is #202 in *The United Methodist Hymnal* or you can look online) with the group and ask a volunteer to read it aloud. The author points us to this carol, noting that it "beautifully and joyfully emphasizes Advent as a time of evangelistic preparation." He suggests that it "points us to the importance of communal hospitality as we await Christ's birth." Invite participants to respond in writing in their journals to some of the following:

- As the author asks, "How might our Christmas celebrations change if we decorated the tree, hung the lights, and wrapped gifts as if love might be a guest in our home?"
- What persons or groups in our congregation—and in our communities—are most in need of receiving a visit from love? In what ways might I exemplify that love?
- The Christmas story, we read, is a story of vulnerability: the vulnerability of a woman giving birth in a stable, the vulnerability of a newborn infant, the vulnerability that follows when powers are threatened, or perceive that they are. Matt Rawle notes that inviting love into our lives as a guest makes us vulnerable, too. How might I live more fully into that vulnerability? Through understanding more clearly that perfection is not a goal of Christmas celebrations? Through eyes that see more clearly the vulnerability of others with less privilege than I have? Through acknowledging that I need others and can embrace community?

As the frenzy of secular holiday preparations increases in the coming week, encourage participants to focus, in their times of devotions and meditation, on love as the guest. Suggest that they center their prayers on more fully inviting love in the person of Jesus Christ into their Advent preparations.

More Activities (Optional)

View a Segment of The Nutcracker

If you have been viewing segments of *The Nutcracker* from the Internet, you may want to have the group view again the battle scenes with the mice. Encourage the group to notice especially the back-and-forth action of the battle.

Explore the Back and Forth of Christmas

The author notes that "sometimes Christmas can seem like a back-and-forth battle." Form pairs or small groups, depending on the size of your group. In each pair or small group, invite participants to briefly describe how they celebrate Christmas morning.

After allowing a few minutes for pairs or groups to share, call everyone's attention to what the author says about how when he married, he and his wife had to accommodate each other's Christmas traditions. Then pose the following questions for the pairs or groups to consider:

- If you are a spouse or a partner, in what ways did you have to alter your Christmas celebration so that both partners' ideas of how Christmas should be celebrated could be accommodated? What, if anything, did each of you have to give up?

- If you are part of a blended family, what changes had to be made to accommodate everyone? How did you decide what changes to make?
- If you are single, how do you tailor your Christmas Day celebration to accommodate other family members?
- In any case, how did you and those you consider family decide which traditions to keep, which to discard, and which to transform in some way?

Debate "The War On Christmas"

Call the group's attention to the three examples the author gives us: a Starbucks cup; "Christmas" versus "winter break"; taking "Christmas" off of sales-rack advertisements. Point out that they serve as a sort of shorthand for what some term "The War on Christmas." Ask for volunteers who will debate the following proposition:

> Resolved: There is a War on Christmas that threatens this sacred holiday.

Form two teams with equal numbers of persons on each team, and arbitrarily assign the affirmative and negative positions. Allow each team a few minutes to discuss their argument and choose a person to present it, as well as one other person to present a short rebuttal speech. Have each team's debater give a two-minute speech presenting their position, with the rest of the participants serving as the audience. Follow the first two speeches with the rebuttal speeches.

Invite the group to debrief the debate. Then discuss:

- The author observes that "sometimes we confuse evangelism with apologetics, the discipline of defending one's faith." Would you categorize the debates around

Christmas as attempts to defend our faith? If so, how effective do you think that strategy is?

- "Sharing the Christian story and inviting people to become a part of it," says Rawle, "will always be more important than defending it." In what ways do your Christmas traditions share the Christian story? How might we be more strategic about doing so?

WRAPPING UP

Remind the group that in discussing the gift of grace freely given, the author points out that something must die in order for us to be born again. He points us to a passage in Isaiah often read as a part of Advent scriptures. Ask a volunteer to read aloud Isaiah 52:7 and chapter 53:4-5a, 8b. Invite the group to consider the following:

In this season of Advent, I will embrace the costly grace of Jesus Christ by letting go of _____.

Invite volunteers who are willing to do so to respond, popcorn style, out loud. Encourage others to reflect in silence.

Remind participants to read Chapter 4 before the last session.

Closing Activity

Light a Candle and Sing a Hymn

Light three of the four candles and sit in silence for a few moments. Then say, "Come, Lord Jesus."

Sing "People, Look East" if you have decided to do so, or simply have the group view a video segment of the carol or read the stanzas aloud together.

Closing Prayer

Pray the following, or a prayer of your choosing:

Come, Lord Jesus. We give thanks that you came to announce God's good news for the world. We thank you, too, that you died and rose again so that we might live into the abundant life you intend. Give us renewed strength as we seek to let go of all that sedates us to the needs of a hurting world. Amen.

Session 4

THE NUTCRACKER:
THE GREATEST GIFT

PLANNING THE SESSION

Session Goals

As a result of conversations and activities connected with this session, group members should explore, through the lens of Scripture, what *The Nutcracker* reveals about the gift of Jesus Christ by beginning to:

- consider the implications of gifts wanted and needed;
- encounter the incarnational work of Advent;
- reflect on incarnational work begun in Advent and anticipated.

Scriptural Foundation

"You will conceive in your womb and bear a son, and you will name him Jesus. He will be great,

*and will be called the Son of the Most High, and
the Lord God will give to him the throne of his
ancestor David. He will reign over the house of
Jacob forever, and of his kingdom there will be no
end. . . ." "The Holy Spirit will come upon you, and
the power of the Most High will overshadow you;
therefore the child to be born will be holy; he will
be called Son of God."*

Luke 1:31-33, 35

*In that region there were shepherds living in the
fields, keeping watch over their flock by night.
Then an angel of the Lord stood before them, and
the glory of the Lord shone around them, and they
were terrified. But the angel said to them, "Do not
be afraid; for see—I am bringing you good news of
great joy for all the people."*

Luke 2:8-10

Special Preparation

- Again have writing materials available for anyone who did not bring a journal.
- Print the questions for small groups for the activity on encountering the incarnational work of Advent on four large sheets of paper or four sections of a board (these questions are provided in the Appendix).
- Decide if you will use any of the optional additional activities. If you will be watching video of the ballet, download selected segments from the Internet and obtain equipment for viewing. For this session, search for short segments from Act 2 showing the festival the Sugar Plum Fairy puts on for Clara, with music and dances from a variety of cultures. For the Advent word-picture activity,

provide drawing or construction paper and fine-lined, colored markers or crayons. Alternatively, to use Wordle, participants will need access to smartphones. To compare versions of "Silent Night," download the two versions from the Internet and obtain equipment for viewing.

- For the closing activity, decide if you will sing several carols, such as "Hark! The Herald Angels Sing," "Silent Night," and "Joy to the World." Most hymnals and Christmas songbooks contain these carols. Arrange for accompaniment, or plan to have the group simply sing a cappella, with no accompaniment to their voices.

- You will again need four Advent candles, either in an Advent wreath or simply standing in a line. Electronic candles are a good alternative if your church has restrictions about lighting conventional candles.

GETTING STARTED

Opening Activity

As participants arrive, welcome them. Ask the group to recall the reflecting question posed by the author in Chapter 3:

- How might our Christmas celebrations change if we decorated the tree, hung the lights, and wrapped gifts as if love might be a guest in our home?

With the understanding that most participants have already decorated their trees and hung the lights and may be well on the way to having the gifts purchased and wrapped, invite volunteers to describe ways, however small, that they were able to welcome love as a guest in the preceding week in the midst of their preparations.

Call the group's attention to the following question the author poses at the beginning of Chapter 4:

- Have you ever wondered why people put trees in their living rooms to celebrate Jesus' birth?

If no one responds, explain that this tradition comes from the sixteenth century, when German Christians began placing trees inside their homes. Encourage participants to add other details, such as the popular story that Martin Luther first added candles to the tree after marveling at the stars outside.

Ask:

- Are there Christmas traditions in your family that originated in the countries or cultures or regions from which you or your ancestors came? If so, what are they?

Remind the group that the author suggests that when the angel in Luke's Gospel says to the shepherds, "I am bringing you good news of great joy for all the people," our perception is being expanded to include God's gift of Jesus to all cultures, peoples, and languages. In this final session, participants will explore the implications of such an affirmation.

Opening Prayer

Pray the following prayer, or one of your own choosing:

Eternal God of love, as we enter these final days of Advent, gather us together into a place of quiet rest. Here in this place, prepare for us a space in which we can contemplate the peace, hope, love, and joy of Advent. Guide us as we seek to find ways to give you thanks for your amazing gift, and prod us as we seek to discern how best to respond. Amen.

LEARNING TOGETHER

Video Study and Discussion

In Chapter 4, we continue the discussion of the gift of Jesus Christ, the embodiment of the gift of God's grace. The nutcracker is a gift Clara didn't ask for and isn't sure she needs. In a similar way, we explore the idea that at times, Jesus might not seem like the gift we want, but he certainly is the gift we need. When the Nutcracker comes back to life following his death in the battle, he takes Clara on a journey to a kingdom filled with people from all corners of the world who celebrate their arrival. Likewise, we affirm that in response to the gift of Jesus Christ, we join together with all peoples and cultures in the work of transforming the world.

After viewing the video segment, discuss some of the following:

- God has given us this gift of the person of Jesus Christ. The one question the author suggests we should ask is: Is this the gift we want? What does Matt Rawle have to say about this question? How do you respond?
- Despite the fact that Clara isn't sure she wants the nutcracker, we hear that this gift is the gift that Clara needs. How do we find out and why?
- Rawle points out that our Christmas traditions vary from family to family, house to house, church to church, and country to country, yet there is unity in the reason for our celebrations. How does *The Nutcracker* story lift up this unity?
- Name a tradition in your own family, one that may be unique to you. How is that tradition grounded in your own family background? What common traditions do you share with others in your church? In your community?

Book and Bible Study and Discussion

Consider the Implications of Gifts Wanted and Needed

Recall for the group that in Session 2, the author discussed in the video segment some friends of his who received gifts for which they had not asked. Just as is the case with Clara and the gift of the nutcracker, these friends were not sure they wanted the gifts, although later they changed their minds. Now Matt Rawle invites us to consider the following:

- Have you ever received exactly what you wanted, but getting what you wanted led to receiving lots of things you didn't?

Invite volunteers who have had this experience to tell about it. Then delve deeper into the idea that sometimes the things we want aren't the things we need, and the things we need aren't what we want, specifically as that idea applies to the gift of Jesus Christ. Discuss some of the following:

- The author tells us that "Jesus fulfills our desire for peace, spiritual nourishment, and the way that leads to life." But "Jesus also asks something of us." What is it?
- What is the relationship between the acts of service, compassion, and justice to which Jesus calls us and salvation? Between these and grace?
- What connections, if any, do you see between these ideas and the fact that in the story, the Nutcracker sacrifices his own life to save Clara and is then transformed by Drosselmeir and brought back to life? What is then the role of the transformed Nutcracker?

Encounter the Incarnational Work of Advent

The author speaks of "God's incarnational work...which began in the humble manger [and] continues today." Form four small groups or pairs, depending on the size of your group. Assign to each pair or group one of the four facets of that incarnational work (peace, hope, love, or joy), and call their attention to the questions posted for their assigned aspect. Ask them to read the scriptures listed and discuss the questions together.

After allowing several minutes for groups or pairs to work, come together in the total group. Give each pair or group the opportunity to report on their conversation, as well as to pose any questions that came up in their discussion.

Reflect on Incarnational Work Begun and Anticipated

Remind the group that we read in the text that in Jesus Christ, the "incarnational work of peace, hope, love, and joy" was established. Yet in reflecting on the world in which we live, we acknowledge that sometimes that work seems muted or even absent. So we pray for these gifts to come into fruition.

Invite the group to engage in the following spiritual exercise of focused meditation. Ask them to find a comfortable position for sitting and to breathe in and out deeply and slowly several times. On the exhale, ask them to visualize breathing out the distractions and the hectic tone and worries of the secular seasonal frenzy. On the inhale, invite them to breathe in a sense of God's presence. After sitting in silence and engaging in deep breathing for one minute, invite them to join in the following:

ALL: **Come, Lord Jesus...grant us peace....**

Leader: Where are the places and who are the peoples most in need of God's shalom?

(Invite participants to name them aloud if they so choose.)

How can I be a part of the incarnational work of peace? *(Pause for silence.)*

ALL: **Come, Lord Jesus... grant us hope....**

Leader: Where are the places and who are the peoples most in need of God's hope?

(Invite participants to name them aloud if they so choose.)
How can I be a part of the incarnational work of hope?
(Pause for silence.)

ALL: **Come, Lord Jesus... grant us love....**

Leader: Where are the places and who are the peoples most in need of God's love?

(Invite participants to name them aloud if they so choose.)
How can I be a part of the incarnational work of love?
(Pause for silence.)

ALL: **Come, Lord Jesus... grant us joy....**

Leader: Where are the places and who are the peoples most in need of God's joy?

(Invite participants to name them aloud if they so choose.)
How can I be a part of the incarnational work of joy?
(Pause for silence.)

Encourage participants in the few days remaining before Christmas to use this focused meditation as a part of their devotional times.

More Activities (Optional)

View a Segment of The Nutcracker

View short segments of the ballet from Act 2 showing the festival the Sugar Plum Fairy puts on for Clara, with music and dances from a variety of cultures. Discuss together:

- Matt Rawle asks us to think about the following: "Have you considered what *The Nutcracker* story might be like if it had been written in South Africa? How would the story change if E. T. A. Hoffman had been Korean? Maybe there would be no nutcracker at all in the story if it took place in Chile." What do you think?

- If you were planning dances that portray a variety of cultures, what cultures not depicted in *The Nutcracker* would you include? If you were the composer for additional dances, what types of music would you pair with a culture's dance?

Create Advent Word Pictures

Invite the group to create word pictures to illustrate the incarnational work exemplified in the words *peace, hope, love,* and *joy.* Form four smaller groups or pairs, depending on the size of your group. Assign one of the four words to each group or pair. Distribute drawing or construction paper and crayons or fine-lined, colored markers. Ask participants to review the information in the chapter about their word, jotting down words or phrases that expand what that word encompasses in Advent. They can also add other words or phrases that come to mind. Encourage each person to form a word picture with some or all of the words or phrases by printing or writing them on the paper, giving more important words larger size, repetition, or stronger colors.

Alternatively, when groups or pairs have typed their list into their phones, they can go to Wordle.net and cut and paste it into the Wordle template to form a word picture.

In the total group, ask each group to display and explain their word pictures.

Compare Versions of "Silent Night"

Participants can explore further the contrasts and intersections between and among the words *peace, hope, love,* and *joy* by comparing and contrasting two versions of "Silent Night." Play the version of "Silent Night" by the David Crowder Band, the version described by Rawle in the text. Then play the version by Simon and Garfunkel titled "Silent Night/7 O'Clock News." Discuss:

- Describe which versions (one or both) embody one or more of the four elements of the work of incarnation.
- In the Simon and Garfunkel version, we hear, gradually increasing in volume, a litany of the bad news of the time. In what ways are those news items echoed in today's news feed? Where, if at all, do you hear evidence that the work of incarnation is absent and needed?
- In contrast, in the David Crowder Band version, it is the volume and tempo of the music that increases. What is the effect of this on the mood of the carol? Which work(s) of incarnation seems most evident at the culmination of the carol?

WRAPPING UP

Give participants the opportunity to name insights they have gleaned from this study, areas they most enjoyed exploring, aspects they would have liked pursuing further, or any lingering questions. Then invite them to respond as they wish, popcorn style, to the following open-ended prompts:

In experiencing the story of *The Nutcracker* through Clara's eyes, I was able to see more clearly my own perspective about God's gift of Jesus by _____.

Drosselmeir revealed himself as a God figure by _____.

In the character of The Nutcracker, I made connections to
Jesus Christ by _____.

To me, The Mouse King and his minions represent _____.

The ending celebration with dancers from across the globe
reminds me that _____.

If participants still have the opportunity to see *The Nutcracker*
ballet live, encourage them to do so. Alternatively, they can find
various versions of the entire ballet online.

Closing Activity

Light a Candle and Sing a Hymn

Light all four candles and sit in silence for a few moments.
Then say, "Come, Lord Jesus." Sing together "Hark! The Herald
Angels Sing," "Silent Night," "Joy to the World," or other carols of
your choice.

Closing Prayer

Pray the following, or a prayer of your choosing:

*Come, Lord Jesus. We welcome you again into our hearts. As the
light of Christmas dawns and begins to shine fully, engage not only
our hearts and minds, but our hands, our feet, and our will to
join in the incarnational work of peace, hope, love, and joy. In the
name of the child born in the manger and crucified on the cross,
Amen.*

APPENDIX

Group 1: Hope

Read Luke 1:26-38. Discuss the following:

- We read that Mary's reaction to her encounter with Gabriel places her "squarely in the tradition of the great prophets from the Hebrew Scriptures." How is the traditional pattern of prophetic call and response reflected in Mary's interactions with Gabriel? What distinguishes this holy interaction from the other prophetic patterns?

- Scripture tells us that Mary allowed herself to be overshadowed by the Holy Spirit. The author observes that it seems "Christmas rather than Christ ... overshadows us this time of year." What does he mean? What aspects of the holiday season overshadow you?

- What does the author suggest should overshadow us as the season culminates in the celebration of Christmas? He notes that "we should be perplexed over God's ... hope." How do you respond?

Group 2: Peace

Read Luke 2:8-20. Discuss the following:

- The story of *The Nutcracker* is told through the eyes of a twelve-year-old girl. How does your perspective—your background and heritage—shape the way you experience the Nativity story? Where is there diversity across cultures and peoples in how we share the Christmas story? Where is there unity?
- The author makes a connection between the incarnational work of hope and the work of peace in Israel's history, exemplified in Psalm 137. Do you think the words of the psalm indicate a longing for peace or for something else? What do God's first words to the people on their eventual return ("Comfort, O comfort my people…") signify?
- What is *shalom*? How does it differ from an absence of conflict? Where, if anywhere, do you see glimpses of shalom in the world today? The author notes that "one way to begin offering *shalom* to the world is through listening to and understanding those who aren't us." Who represents the "other" to you? What ways can you suggest to listen to and better understand those persons' perspectives?

Group 3: Love

Read Luke 1:26-38. Discuss the following:

- After noting the words of the angel Gabriel to Mary, Matt Rawle observes that it's not that everything is possible. It's that nothing is impossible. What distinction is he making here? Do you agree? Why or why not?

- We read that one of the pictures the Rawle family has placed prominently in their home is a sign that reads, "Where there is love, there are miracles." What is the sign a reminder of? In relating the story of a friend estranged from his father, who was diagnosed with cancer, Rawle notes that one could make the argument that a miracle didn't happen, but that something miraculous did move between them. What happened between the two? How was healing involved?

Group 4: Joy

Read Luke 1:26-38. Discuss the following:

- The Christmas story is described in this chapter as a dance. What does the author mean? He notes that the "story about Jesus' birth is a story about a God with a face," and "this God with a face offers us a beautiful tension." What is the tension?
- Rawle relates the story of a Christmas Eve when he departed from the traditional singing of "Silent Night," replacing it instead with the David Crowder Band version. What does this version of the carol serve as a reminder of for the author?
- We are told that the first word Jesus speaks in the Gospels is "Why." What does the author mean when he observes that "Jesus begins with a human 'why,' and then ends with a divine unlocking of mystery"? If we are indeed partners with God in this dance, then what does that mean for us?
- How does Rawle's daughter define joy? How would you?

35639674R00037

Printed in Great Britain
by Amazon